KU-688-306

THE CHANGING FACE OF THE
NETHERLANDS

Text and Photographs
by DAVID SIMSON

C 03 0149984

HODDER
Wayland

an imprint of Hodder Children's Books

© 2004 White-Thomson Publishing Ltd

Produced for Hodder Wayland by
White-Thomson Publishing Ltd
2/3 St Andrew's Place
Lewes BN7 1UP

Editor: Elaine Fuoco-Lang
Designer: Clare Nicholas
Concept Design: Chris Halls, Mind's Eye Design
Proofreader: Alison Cooper
Consultant: Marc A. Price

First published in Great Britain in 2004 by Hodder Wayland, an imprint of
Hodder Children's Books.
This paperback edition published in 2005

The right of David Simson to be identified as the author of this work has
been asserted by him in accordance with the Copyright, Designs and
Patents Act 1988.

All rights reserved. Apart from any use permitted under UK copyright law, this
publication may only be reproduced, stored or transmitted, in any form, or by
any means with prior permission in writing of the publishers or in the case of
reprographic production in accordance with the terms of licences issued by the
Copyright Licensing Agency.

WEST DUNBARTONSHIRE LIBRARIES	
C030149984	
CAW	30/09/2005
J949.2073	£6.99
FA	

British Library Cataloguing in Publication Data
Simson, David
  The Changing Face of the Netherlands
  1. Human geography – Netherlands - Juvenile literature
  2. Netherlands - History - 1945 - Juvenile Literature
  3. Netherlands - Social life and customs - Juvenile literature
  I. Title II. Netherlands
  949.2'073

ISBN 0 7502 4811 4

Printed in China

Hodder Children's Books
A division of Hodder Headline Limited
338 Euston Road, London NW1 3BH

The website addresses (URLs) included in this book were valid at the time of
going to press. However, because of the nature of the Internet, it is possible
that some addresses may have changed, or sites may have changed or closed
down since publication. While the author and Publisher regret any
inconvenience this may cause readers, no responsibility for any such changes
can be accepted by the author, the Packager or the Publisher.

Acknowledgements
The publishers would like to thank
the following for their contributions
to this book: Rob Bowden – statistics
research; Peter Bull – map
illustration; Nick Hawken – statistics
panel illustrations. All photographs
are by DASPHOTOGB@aol.com
(David Simson B-6940 Septon).

Contents

Rotterdam – the Reborn City

Rotterdam, now a bustling city of 600,000 people, was once a small settlement built on the River Rotte around 1270 CE. It grew slowly through the centuries – in the 1400s for instance, whilst neighbouring Delft was an important city, Rotterdam was still a very small town. In 1872 a new canal was built which linked the great rivers of Europe and flowed through Rotterdam to the sea. This canal made the city an important centre for trade and industry, and it became very wealthy.

In 1940 Hitler invaded the Netherlands. Most of the buildings in Rotterdam were completely demolished. At the end of the Second World War, in 1945, Het Schielandshuis was one of the only historic buildings left standing. Originally a government office, it is now Rotterdam's Historic Museum.

Rotterdam was entirely rebuilt after the war. Its modern architecture, such as the Erasmus Bridge and the Cubehouses, has become world-renowned. Exciting shopping malls have replaced more traditional shopping areas and the world's largest port, the Europoort, has been built at Rotterdam.

Due to its central position in Europe and excellent transport links, Rotterdam has become a centre for Internet companies and other businesses. The Dutch-owned multinational company Unilever has its headquarters in the city. Several Shell oil refineries and well-known companies such as IBM, Toshiba and Microsoft all do business here. As the European Union expands, Rotterdam – like the Netherlands itself – should enjoy continued prosperity.

▲ *The Rotterdam Historic Museum,* Het Schielandshuis *is a reminder of the people of Rotterdam's resilience in times of adversity.*

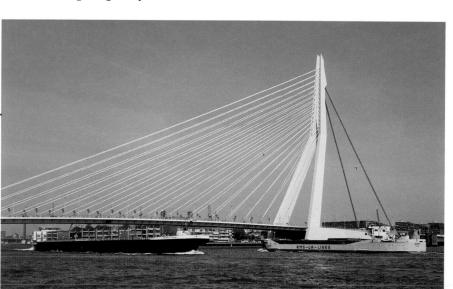

◄ *The Erasmus Bridge, an example of the stunning modern architecture in the city of Rotterdam. Barges and ships travel non-stop between the Europoort on the coast through the city of Rotterdam to the heartlands of Europe.*

Map labels:

Wadden Islands
Ameland
Terschelling
Nes
Waddensee Coast
Texel
Groningen
FRIESLAND
Callantsoog
NETHERLANDS
IJsselmeer
Meppel
NORTH SEA
Alkmaar
Urk
Edam
Volendam
Lelystad
Zwolle
Haarlem
Amsterdam
FLEVOLAND
Aalsmeer
Enschede
Leiden
Nieuwkoop
UTRECHT
The Hague
Utrecht
Delft
Gouda
Arnhem
Europoort
Rotterdam
Waal
Rhine
Dordrecht
Maas
Brouwersdam
Colijnsplaat
Etten-Leur
Breda
Tilburg
ZEELAND
Eindhoven
Schelde
LIMBURG
BELGIUM
GERMANY
Meerssen
Maastricht
Vaalserberg 322m
0 100 km
0 50 miles
N

▲ *This map shows the main geographical features of the Netherlands as well as most of the places mentioned in this book.*

THE NETHERLANDS: KEY FACTS

Area: 41,526 sq km, 33,948 sq km excluding water

Population: 16.07 million

Population density: 473 people per sq km

Capital city: Amsterdam

Other main cities: The Hague, Utrecht, Eindhoven, Tilburg

Lowest point: Zuidplaspolder –7 m

Highest point: Vaalserberg 322 m

Longest river: Maas 314 km

Total length of waterways: 5,046 km (3,745 km are canals)

Main language: Dutch

Major religions: Roman Catholic 31 per cent, Protestant 21 per cent, Muslim 4.4 per cent, other 3.6 per cent, unaffiliated 40 per cent

Currency: Euro

2 Past Times

The people and language of the Netherlands are known in English as 'Dutch'. Dutch comes from the German word for German, 'Deutsch'. The majority of the Dutch population is of Germanic heritage. In the Netherlands they refer to themselves as 'Nederlanders' and their language as 'Nederlands'.

The area was first inhabited by Celtic and Germanic tribes. In the 1400s, the area came under the control of the Austro-Hungarian Empire, and in the 1500s it was taken over by Spain. A war of independence from Spain was waged for 80 years and independence was finally won in 1648. The years 1600–1700 are known as the 'Golden Age' of Dutch history. This was a period of unusual wealth and freedom for the country. Belgium and Luxembourg were part of the Netherlands at that time and the country became a 'colonial power', meaning that it controlled other less powerful countries in the third world where it had trade interests.

▲ The Royal Palace in Amsterdam was first used as the City Hall in 1655 to reflect the wealth of the city.

▼ Even though the capital of the Netherlands is Amsterdam, the Binnenhof, the historic Dutch Parliament Buildings, have been in The Hague since the 1500s.

From 1795 the Netherlands came under the control of France and in 1815 independence was restored. The Netherlands stayed neutral during the First World War (1914-18), but was invaded by Nazi Germany during the Second World War (1939-45). Although the Netherlands had a tradition of neutrality, in 1949 it joined NATO and in 1957 it became one of the founding members of the European Economic Community.

Today the Netherlands' government is a constitutional monarchy. This means that although there is a monarch (Queen Beatrix since 1980) the country is a democracy.

▶ *Queen Beatrix attending the signing of the Treaty of Maastricht in 1991.*

IN THEIR OWN WORDS

'My name is Jelle van der Beek. I am 16 and go to school in Tilburg. Sometimes I work in a trendy clothes boutique in the city to make pocket money. My favourite subject is history. In Dutch schools, European and international history is taught alongside Dutch history. It gives us a wider view of the world. Many people do not know for instance that New York's original name was New Amsterdam because the Dutch were the first people to settle there. And Harlem was named after Haarlem in Holland. The first European navigator to discover New Zealand was a Dutchmen called Abel Tasman, not Captain Cook. Tasmania and the Tasman sea were named after him. New Zealand was named after the Dutch province of Zeeland.'

Landscape and Climate

The Netherlands is bordered by Belgium, Germany and the North Sea, and it has a total land area of 33,948 sq km. It is a very flat, low-lying country. The estuaries of three major rivers, the Rhine, the Maas and the Schelde, are in the Netherlands, and the land is criss-crossed by rivers, canals and drainage ditches. Thirty per cent of the land is below sea level, which means that floods are a great danger. Huge sand dunes help to protect the land. Where there are no dunes, artificial sea defences have been built, such as the 30 km *Afsluitdijk* (shut-off dike), the North Holland Seawall (running south of Den Helder) and sea locks like the Zeeland Delta Project. A complicated drainage system helps to prevent flooding inland on the polders.

▼ *Coarse grasses are grown on the natural sand dunes at Brouwersdam in the Zeeland Delta region to hold the sand in place.*

The polders

Polders make up large areas of the Netherlands. A polder is an area of land that has been reclaimed from the sea. Making a polder is a very long process. The first stage is to build a dike to enclose a large area of the sea. Water is pumped out until the area is completely dry. In the past windmills were used for this task. Coarse grasses are then

IN THEIR OWN WORDS

'My name is Binne Kunnen and I'm 61 years old. I am originally a farmer's son from Friesland. I am a farmer now but live in another province called Flevoland. Forty years ago Flevoland did not exist because it was under water. This area used to be a large bay in the North Sea called the Zuiderzee. After the building of the *Afsluitdijk* it became a large lake called the IJsselmeer. It has been gradually dried out to become the largest polder in the Netherlands, large enough to become a new province. If we had been standing here forty years ago, we would have been on the seabed under more than fifteen feet of water! Today we grow wheat, onions, potatoes, carrots, and tulips of course.'

planted, which help to firm the soil and reduce the salt content. This process takes several years, and fertilizers must be used before the land can be used as productive farmland. Sections of the IJsselmeer have been dried out to create a new province of the Netherlands, known as Flevoland.

▼ *New housing estates, some with their own boat jetties, have been built in the new city of Lelystad, on the large Flevoland polder.*

Islands and heathlands

Along the full length of the North Sea coast (643 km) there are beautiful sandy beaches backed by high dunes and artificial sea defences. Just off the north coast there is a line of low sandy islands called the Wadden Islands. These are important breeding sites for birds and they are also popular with holidaymakers.

The Hoge Veluwe, near the eastern border with Germany, is the Netherlands' largest national park. It is an area of forest, sand and heathland, where red deer and wild boar can sometimes be spotted.

The hilly south

Limburg in the south-east of the country is quite different from the rest of the Netherlands, because it is hilly. The two countries that border the Netherlands, Germany and Belgium, meet here at a point called the *Drielandenpunt* 'Point of Three Countries'. This is the highest point in the Netherlands but it is only 322 m high.

▲ *An avenue of large oak trees in the Hoge Veluwe National Park in the eastern Netherlands.*

▼ *The hilly orchard and meadow land of South Limburg.*

IN THEIR OWN WORDS

'I'm Sander Kroonen – I am 14. I live at Vaals on the border of both Germany and Belgium. The three borders meet here at the *Drielandenpunt*, the highest point in the Netherlands. It is only 332 metres high. My mum comes from here. My father is actually Belgian. He now works in Aachen, a city in neighbouring Germany, only fifteen minutes away. The *Drielandenpunt* is a great place to go exploring. Only a few years ago you couldn't go there without a passport or identity papers. There used to be a manned border control now there isn't even a border post. Everyone used to have to change money. Now we all use the euro.'

The Netherlands Antilles

The Netherlands Antilles is a group of tropical islands in the Caribbean. Aruba, Bonaire and Curaçao are flat, dry islands off the Venezuelan coast. Sint Eustatius, Saba and part of Sint Maarten in the Leeward Islands are volcanic and mountainous. The Antilles were once colonies of the Netherlands. Today, they have complete control of their internal affairs although the Netherlands is responsible for their defence and foreign affairs.

▶ *The main beach at Philipsburg on Sint Maarten in the Netherlands Antilles. This island is part French and part Dutch.*

Mild, wet and windy

The climate of the Netherlands is typical of the northern European North Sea coast. It is mild and very wet, with a yearly average rainfall of 76 mm. In the summer the temperatures rarely rise very high, and mid-winter temperatures usually remain above zero. In north Holland the average January temperature is 5 °C, and in July the average is 21 °C. Further inland, the weather tends to be drier with some snow in the winter and higher temperatures in the summer.

▲ *The view of windmills and canals has become the accepted typical Dutch landscape, although now modern postards often have wind turbines on them.*

Winds blow in from the sea and sweep across the flat countryside. When there is no wind, a thick fog often covers the entire country. In summer this usually clears by late morning and the rest of the day is beautifully sunny. In winter, a misty morning usually turns into a grey, dull day.

◄ *This is the Kite Festival on Scheveningen Beach near The Hague. It takes advantage of the sandy beaches and the almost constant windy conditions.*

Changing climate

The climate of the Netherlands has changed over the years – it has been getting much warmer. There is a famous 200-km ice-skating race, called the Elfstedentocht, which takes place on the canals through eleven towns in Friesland and attracts up to 18,000 people from all over the country. At the end of the nineteenth century this race took place almost every year, once the canals had frozen solid. These days the canals don't freeze up like they used to, and now the race only takes place about once every five years.

► *The Sint Servaas Bridge over the River Maas at Maastricht. In the south, the weather tends to be more continental with colder winters but also hotter summers.*

IN THEIR OWN WORDS

'My name is René Waleson. I am 40 and am a technician at one of the Rotterdam Water Board's plants. This plant cleans all the household and factory wastewater from a large area of Rotterdam. After cleaning, this water is put back in the river. We actually clean 100 million litres of wastewater everyday. That is the same as 35 Olympic swimming pools. The Water Boards do a very important job. They control water pollution, the construction and maintenance of dikes, and general water levels to prevent flooding. In the floods of January 1953, thousands of people died when water rose too high and flooded large areas of the country. It is the Water Board's job to prevent this from happening ever again.'

4 Natural Resources

Gas and oil

Gas and oil were discovered offshore in the late 1960s. Many industries have developed to process the fuel or make oil-based products such as plastics and textiles. Ninety-five per cent of all household energy requirements in the Netherlands are provided by natural gas. The country also makes more money from exporting gas than from any other product – 50 per cent of all Dutch gas is exported.

◀ A North Sea oil rig being repaired in Rotterdam's Europoort. Once repaired, the rig will then be towed out to sea again to extract oil and gas from the seabed of the North Sea.

▼ A large wind farm near Zurich in Friesland. Wind power is considered very important in this windy country, even though it only produces a very small part of the nation's energy requirements.

Wind power

Wind power has been an important energy source in the Netherlands for centuries. Windmills were used in the past, for pumping out water from the polders, grinding wheat, pulping paper and making linseed oil. Now wind turbines are used to produce electricity for the nation and there are many wind farms.

IN THEIR OWN WORDS

'I'm Femke Klapwijk. I am 14 and I go to the Goes Lyceum school. But I live here in Colijnsplaat, a beautiful little Zeeland fishing village with fishing boats and windmills. It used to be on the sea but then the Delta Project Sea Locks were built, and now the trawlers have to go through a lock to get to the sea. My father is a trawlerman and works out in the North Sea every day. He mainly fishes for sole, plaice, dab, cod and eels. At the weekends I work at a quayside fishmongers. Many people from as far away as Rotterdam come and buy fish here. We sell a lot of mussels too, mainly to Belgians who come across the ferry at Breskens.'

Fishing

The fishing industry has been in difficulties in recent years. The European Union restricts the amount (the quota) of fish that each country can catch. The quotas are being reduced because of concerns that the numbers of fish in the North Sea are falling. Pollution is one of the causes of this. However, the Zeeland mussel industry is thriving. This is mainly due to a healthy demand in northern Europe, particularly in Belgium, where a plate of mussels is a favourite national dish.

▼ Urk, once an island, was a famous seaport for over 700 years. Now the port is more than 50 kilometres inland, on the IJsselmeer, a long way from open sea.

Dairy and livestock

Almost half the land area of the Netherlands is used for farming, with most of this being used for raising livestock. The Dutch dairy industry is one of the most efficient in the world, producing large quantities of milk, butter and cheese, as well as many by-products, such as yoghurt, powdered milk and ingredients for factory-produced ready-made meals. Beef, pork and chicken are also important farm products in the Netherlands.

▲ *Cheeses being sold at Alkmaar. In the Netherlands, there is plenty of fresh milk, butter and cheese.*

◀ *There are many new farming practices, from the use of computer-run greenhouses and eco farming to the rearing of bison, as on this farm in the south of the country.*

Crops and horticulture

The Netherlands is famous for its tulips and the flower industry is one of the most advanced and profitable in the world. Flowers from the Netherlands are flown daily to flower markets worldwide. Its success is based on the use of the latest scientific techniques and automated production, which ensures that the plants get exactly the growing conditions they need. This is also the case with market gardening. Millions of computer-controlled greenhouses in

the Westland produce high-quality vegetables all year round, even outside their normal growing season. The Netherlands achieves some of the highest yields in fruit, flowers and vegetables of any country in the world.

New crops such as rapeseed, which is used to produce vegetable oil, have been introduced in arable farming. There is a move towards more organic farming and the use of genetically-engineered crops is an important new development.

▲ *The Netherlands has a great horticultural industry. These flowers will be sold at a flower auction in Aalsmeer, where the largest and most successful flower auctions in the world are held.*

IN THEIR OWN WORDS

'I'm Albert Buining. I'm 35 and I work as a security man at the famous Aalsmeer Flower Auction, the largest in the world. It is a strange auction. Instead of the price going up, it starts high and goes down. Then the buyer presses his bell when he wants to purchase that batch of flowers. It is very exciting. If you press your bell too late you lose the flowers to another buyer. If you press it too early, you pay too much. Then the flowers are delivered all over the world, many by air. Apart from general security, we also look after the many tourists that visit us to see the auction for themselves.'

The Changing Environment

Recycling in industry

The need to recycle, reprocess and reuse materials is being tackled very seriously. It is changing the lifestyle of the Dutch as they enter the twenty-first century. The Dutch government has passed many laws to try to stop industries dumping toxic and non-toxic waste. There is a determined effort to get industry to use reprocessed materials. In every town there is a centre where reclaimed building materials are sold to the building trade. Recycled materials are used for road surfacing.

▲ *Fastfood outlets take cleaning both in and around their establishments very seriously. Here in Flevoland, an employee even clears nearby forestland of rubbish.*

Recycling at home

There are 'eco taxes' on any product that is considered to be bad for the environment. People have to pay a deposit on bottles, even plastic ones, which they get back if they return the empty bottles to the shop. On many household machines like vacuum cleaners there is now a 'reprocessing deposit', which you get back if you return it to the store when the machine no longer works or is out of fashion. Many shops have collection boxes for old batteries and other shops no longer give out free plastic bags. People are obliged to sort and separate their waste at home so that the different materials can be recycled.

▶ *Home waste is sorted out into recycleable material, bio-degradable items and general waste.*

Reuse

Charity shops recycle anything from clothes to furniture. *Snuffelmarkt* or jumble sales and street markets are good places to find second-hand goods, and many town councils have stores where they resell items thrown out in the rubbish. On Koninginnedag (Queen's Day), which is 30 April, everyone in the country is invited to sell things they don't need in front of their house, turning the whole country into a massive flea market.

▶ *A second-hand street market near Callantsoog in North Holland.*

IN THEIR OWN WORDS

'My name is Marloes Wolter, I am a 25-year-old teacher. In the Netherlands ecology is taken very seriously. There are all types of new ideas. A recent one is the 'can catcher'. This is a net on the side of country roads, which are specially designed so that walkers, cyclists and particularly car drivers can throw in their rubbish. In many countries, drivers often throw rubbish into the hedgerows and grass verges! Most people in the Netherlands love to exercise in the country so this will help to keep our countryside clean and tidy.'

Traffic congestion

The Netherlands is a densely populated country with a high percentage of car owners. Traffic jams are a major problem, especially in the Randstad, the name given to the region that includes the major cities of Amsterdam, Rotterdam, The Hague and Utrecht. The government is finding some solutions by creating a very efficient public transport system of trams, trains and buses. Vehicles have been banned from the centres of many cities, towns and villages, people mainly use bicycles to get around. But there is still much that can be done to ease traffic congestion.

▲ *Although the roads are busy the volume of traffic would be greater without the good public transport system.*

Air pollution

Lead petrol is no longer sold. Coal is no longer used to heat people's homes. Much of the transport system is powered by electricity, which is less polluting than diesel or petrol. However, air pollution remains a problem. The main culprits are the many traffic jams, the jet aircraft overhead, gas-burning power stations, the factories, and finally the pollution that drifts in from neighbouring countries.

Water pollution

The Netherlands has severe problems with water pollution. Large contaminated rivers flow into the country but the Dutch make every effort to clean polluted and waste waters. The excessive use of chemical fertilizers in farming leads to nitrate contamination. The livestock industry produces nearly 100 million tonnes of animal manure a year. These quantities make the soil less fertile and also poison the groundwater. Manure puts nitrogen into the soil and the

▲ *Schiphol International Airport is Holland's main international airport, which is amongst the busiest in Europe. There are also airports in most towns and cities, which cause air pollution.*

◄ *Many Dutch factories, which use river water for cooling machinery, actually record cleaner water leaving the plant than when it arrives. Much of the pollution seen in the Netherlands arrives from elsewhere.*

groundwater, which in small quantities is good for the fertility of plants. However, in large doses it becomes toxic, killing plant life and destroying the general enviroment. Being one of the most densely populated countries in the world does take its toll. The larger the population, the more pollutants and waste water are produced. The smaller the area, the more severe these problems become.

IN THEIR OWN WORDS

'My name is Maria Sumaryanto. I am 54 years old and work in Dordrecht. My husband and I don't see any point in getting a car. Here in the Netherlands, the transport system is very good. I go to work on my bicycle – good for my health and more economical. All around Dordrecht there are rivers and canals. Many people use the fast ferries. My husband works at Schiphol Airport. This is quite far – nearly 100 miles by road there and back. On the train, it takes just over an hour one-way. In nearby Rotterdam, there are the trams and the European high-speed train. People are beginning to change. They realize that you do not need a car here.'

Conserving the cities

Even though the Dutch love the
countryside, the garden and their
animals, most are city dwellers.
Pressure of space has forced them
into constructing apartment blocks,
but efforts are made to ensure that
modern building projects do not spoil
the appearance of the many beautiful
old towns and cities. They have tried
to avoid large-scale building
developments in the countryside
and here there are quaint old
farmhouses, tollhouses and windmills.
House buyers can choose between
the steep-staired traditional Dutch houses, modern
detached and semi-detached houses or houseboats,
which line rivers and canals throughout the country.

▲ *Life on a barge is a popular
way to live.*

Protecting the countryside

Conserving natural environments in the
Netherlands has not been easy because of
the dense population and the pressure on
land. The Drielandenpunt and the Sint
Pietersberg hills in Limburg have a rural
charm of their own, and there are beautiful
lakeland areas such as the IJsselmeer, the
Loosdrechtseplassen and the
Reeuwijkseplassen. Great care has been
taken to conserve these country areas as
well as the sand dunes of the North Sea
coast, which have been preserved and
strengthened as natural sea defences.

▶ *The scenery in the Biesbosch National Park
is one of the stunning natural resources
of the Netherlands.*

The Hoge Veluwe National Park in the east of the country with its sand and heathland is a haven for wildlife. Another national park is the Biesbosch National Park, 7,000 hectares of delta near Dordrecht. Finally, there are the mudflats and delta areas of Zeeland, which are important reserves for migrating birds.

▶ *At the Seal Sanctuary on the Wadden island of Texel, North Sea seals that are diseased or injured are cared for. Most are eventually returned to the wild.*

IN THEIR OWN WORDS

'I'm Elke Koster. I am 30 and work at the Seal Sanctuary at Pieterburen on the Waddensee coast. Our charity has contacts all along the Dutch coastline and in the Frisian Islands. They locate seals in distress. They bring them to us at Pieterburen. Seals in the North Sea suffer in many ways. Many are injured by passing ships in one of the busiest most polluted seaways in the world. Seals also suffer from viruses and disease. Many tourists come and visit us here, to see the seals and our hospital where we treat them. We often have baby seals that have been washed up on the beaches during the winter storms, which in the North Sea can be very severe.'

6 The Changing Population

The most noticeable change in the population over the last few decades is family size – it is getting smaller. There are several reasons for this. Most women now work outside the home and choose to have fewer children so that they can combine family life with a career. Also, as bringing up children can be expensive people choose to have fewer children so that they can afford to maintain a good standard of living.

The other great change is that people are living to a much older age. A likely reason for this is an excellent health system. The high standard of living is also an important factor: in general, people have good housing, good working conditions and good diets, which all help to keep the population healthy into old age.

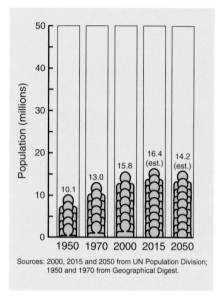

Sources: 2000, 2015 and 2050 from UN Population Division; 1950 and 1970 from Geographical Digest.

▲ *The population of the Netherlands is set to be less in 2050 than it was in 2000.*

◀ *Many women balance family life with a career.*

Caring for the ageing population

The effect of the fall in family size and increased life expectancy is that there are fewer young people and many more in the elderly age group. This will cause serious problems for the country in the future because the healthcare and social benefits provided by the government are paid for by taxes collected from working people. The cost of caring for the ageing population is increasing but the number of young people at work and paying taxes is falling. The government is trying to tackle this problem by reducing the health and social benefits it provides. It is also trying to increase the size of the working population by bringing in workers from overseas.

▶ *There are not enough trained nurses and doctors. Quite a few nurses and doctors now come from African and Asian countries.*

IN THEIR OWN WORDS

'I'm Koen van der Bogt. I'm 21 years old and come from Nieuwkoop. I am studying medicine at the University of Leiden. It takes four years to become a doctor before one specializes. To become a surgeon it takes a total of ten years. I haven't decided on which branch of medicine I would like to follow – maybe I will go into geriatrics. This is caring for old people. There will be more and more need for specialists in this field as our population gets older and older. Generally there are too few doctors and nurses in the Netherlands and pay has not kept up with other professions, so doctors are not happy at the moment.'

Immigration

Over 80 per cent of the population of the Netherlands is of Dutch origin but since the Second World War immigrants have come to the country from many different regions of the world. In the 1940s and 1950s most immigrants came from the former Dutch colonies in the Far East (Indonesia), South America (Surinam), and some from the Netherlands Antilles (Caribbean). In the 1950s immigrants started arriving from Italy and Spain but many of them returned to their homeland, often after retirement. The 1970s saw the arrival of Turkish and Moroccan immigrants, who decided to stay. In the 1980s and 1990s it was the turn of the people from Eastern Europe. Recently immigrants have been arriving from countries as diverse as Algeria, Iraq, Pakistan, Rwanda, Ethiopia and the ex-Soviet republics. Out of a population of over 16 million, there are just under 3 million immigrants.

▼ *There is a large Muslim community, mainly of Turkish and North African origin, living throughout the Netherlands. Here a large group of Turkish immigrants buy material at a market stall.*

IN THEIR OWN WORDS

'My name is Maria Soerjaman. I am 19 and I work in an office at Breda in Brabant. My grandparents are Indonesian. They emigrated to Surinam in South America, then a Dutch colony. I was born in Surinam. Then my family emigrated once again, this time to Holland. Indonesian families have been in the Netherlands such a long time now that we are considered Dutch. I have never had any problems being Indonesian, but maybe that is because I live in a middle-class town. Racism is supposed to be on the increase in cities with a large Muslim population. However the Netherlands is generally a successfully integrated multi-racial society. Many of the famous Dutch footballers are from the ethnic minorities.'

There are now 40,000 legal immigrants who come to the Netherlands annually, but many more arrive illegally. Because of strict controls in the workplace, most of these illegal immigrants are unable to find work, and eventually leave for other European Union countries, where it is easier to find asylum and work. Those who stay legally are boosting a declining population, as their families are traditionally larger. Race relations in the Netherlands are better than in most of the neighbouring European countries.

▶ *This is Rotterdam's largest mosque, the Mevlana mosque, on the west side of the city. Here Rotterdam's Turkish and North African communities congregate for prayers.*

7

Changes at Home

Changes in family life

As recently as 1970 wives in many Dutch families looked after the home and the family. Now more and more women work outside the home and the husband and wife share household tasks.

The divorce rate in the Netherlands has shot up in the last twenty years, as it has in much of the developed world, and it is now one of the highest in the world. It is particularly high among people aged over 50. Economic independence and a 'want to be free' life-style are contributing factors. Possibly because the idea of family is still a very important concept in this country, people often choose to divorce after their children have left home.

There is an increase in single parent families, but in the Netherlands this is mainly caused by divorces and not by teenage pregnancies, as in many other developed countries. The teenage pregnancy rate is said to be much lower than that of other countries due to the excellent school sex-education programme.

More and more people are deciding simply to live together and not to marry at all. Some marry at a much later age, or when they choose to have children.

▲ *Being a single parent in the Netherlands is on the increase.*

◀ *A family on a cycling holiday at Nes on Ameland, one of the Frisian Islands. This is a popular holiday destination with families who have small children, as there are cycle paths, cycle traffic lights and free bike parking areas which makes this a safe and healthy holiday.*

High house prices

The price of houses in the Netherlands has risen so much that young people find it very difficult to afford their first home. Even couples who are both working have difficulty getting a mortgage. As a result, young working adults often live with their parents until they are able to buy their own house or afford a reasonable rent.

There have always been government controls on the rents that landlords can charge and this keeps most rented accommodation affordable. It is not uncommon for Dutch people to rent for their entire life.

▶ *This is a typical apartment block in Breda, a small town in North Brabant. In recent years house prices have increased dramatically throughout the Netherlands.*

IN THEIR OWN WORDS

'Hi my name is Leo Duitsch and I was born in the city of Groningen in the Netherlands. My parents emigrated to Australia when I was 17 years old. My mum and dad then divorced, which is an unfortunate trend in this country. I decided to go back to the Netherlands for a holiday. I had such a great time, I decided to stay even though I was far away from my family. I now own my own business, a typical Dutch snack bar called 'de Hunze'. It is only a few streets away from where I was born! My father has also returned to the Netherlands.'

Health issues

The Dutch health system is of a high standard. Everyone must have medical insurance, either from the state or private companies. Hospitals are excellent. Generally, the Dutch people are fairly fit as shown by their high life expectancy. People in all age groups use bicycles to get around and this helps to keep them healthy. However, their intake of dairy foods, chips and meat means that there is a high rate of heart disease. Also, the high consumption of tobacco and alcohol causes serious medical problems.

Eating habits

Traditional Dutch family meals are varied and healthy. At breakfast the table is set out with many kinds of bread, butter, boiled eggs, cold meats, cheeses, chocolate bits (*hagelslag*), preserves, and even chocolate spread. There is always a pot of hot strong coffee. Lunch is very similar to breakfast. Workers usually eat sandwiches. The early evening meal is the largest meal of the day. This often includes a large plate of cooked meat with vegetables and apple sauce, followed by a dessert. Traditionally, lunch was the largest meal, but this has changed over the years, reflecting the modern lifestyle of working couples doing office jobs (i.e. less physical work).

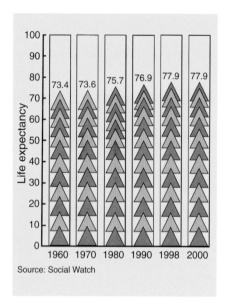

Source: Social Watch

▲ *Life expectancy in the Netherlands is high.*

◄ *Street cafés in Amsterdam are very popular. A typical snack would be an* Uitsmijter *(an open sandwich served with a fried egg on top).*

Eating out might involve downing a whole cured raw herring in the marketplace, with possibly some smoked eels or grey shrimps. Then there are all kinds of sandwiches, called *broodjes* and *uitsmijters* (served open with a fried egg on top). Cakes and coffee are always a favourite. Going out to a restaurant often means going for an Italian meal or having a *rijsttafel* (an assortment of specialities from South-east Asia) in the local Indonesian restaurant. American fast-food shops and the snackbar (*frituur*), a local snack bar serving chips and a range of factory-made snacks, are also popular.

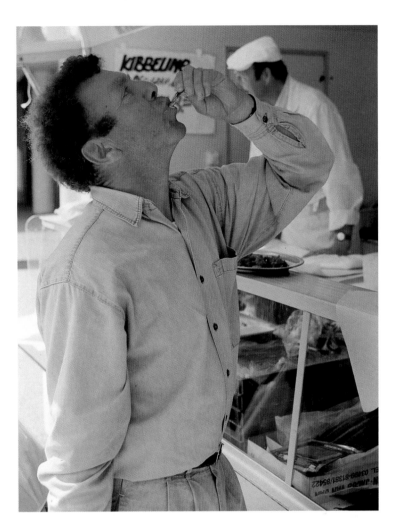

▶ *A favourite Dutch snack is to eat a cured raw herring – swallowed whole. Other seafood favourites are eels, grey shrimps, calamaris, mussels and smoked fish.*

IN THEIR OWN WORDS

'I am Surinder Kumar and am 45 years old. I am a Sikh from India. I have been living in the Netherlands for twenty years. For the last nine years I have owned an Indian restaurant in Breda, specializing in Indian and Surinam dishes. We decided to make Surinam dishes too because of the number of Surinam people who live here in Breda. Surinam people are mixed race, black, white, Indian and Indonesian peoples. They love roti – meat in a huge dough envelope. My restaurant is always busy; we do a lot of take-away business for students and families.'

Education

In the Netherlands there is a system of streamlined education, which means that students are put into separate schools depending on their intellectual level. These are assessed by a series of exams. The system generally achieves high standards.

Pupils from four to twelve years of age attend primary school. After primary school, students are tested for one of the four types of secondary school (higher and lower level) preparing students for technical schools (to study anything from hairdressing to car maintenance), one general school, and one that eventually prepares students for university.

Apprenticeship remains a crucial part of vocational education, when students will be working in industry but also studying at school. For example, a building student will study for four days and work for two days on a construction site. The general school gives a good overall education. This is for students who are not aiming at further education or are unable to and want to enter the workforce as soon as possible without any specialization. Further education is available at fourteen regular universities, fifty universities of professional education and fifteen international education institutes where all courses are conducted in English.

▲ *The number of students attending university, like this one at Rotterdam, has risen in recent years.*

◄ *A professor in car mechanics at a technical school in Wyck teaches a student car maintenance.*

English is very important as a second language. Dutch teenagers use many English words in their daily vocabulary. In some European countries, especially France and Germany, there is concern about the increasing use of English and it is seen as a threat to the national culture and language. However, it is not generally regarded as a problem in the Netherlands. Most Dutch people speak English with some fluency and they often speak several languages. At school everyone takes English and at least one other European language, usually French or German. The Dutch are usually better at German, as Dutch and German are quite similar in many ways.

▶ *Three friends at Groningen University return from an English Language Club to their flats in the city.*

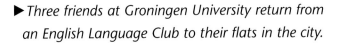

IN THEIR OWN WORDS

'I am Stephan van Keulen, I am 19 and I come from Den Helder in North Holland. I want to study computer science at the Delft University, one of the best in the world, and then go on to study advanced computer studies in the United States. I already have my own business. At 14, I worked at a local computer shop and then two years later I started my own business designing websites. My parents are both computer literate, and they helped me get started. My father is in the Navy and mum runs my office. Computers have changed the way we live in the Netherlands. My business has made quite a lot of money. This will help me during my studies in Delft and America.'

Religion

Christianity is the main religion and for centuries the country has been divided into the mainly Catholic south and mostly Protestant north. The number of people belonging to either religion has fallen, and many Dutch people are now indifferent to religion of any kind. Some have started following exotic religious sects such as Hare Krishna as almost a 'lifestyle' choice. Immigrants have brought into the country new religious influences. There are more than 500,000 practising Muslims and most large cities have at least one mosque.

   Amsterdam once had one of the largest Jewish communities in Europe but almost the entire Jewish population of the Netherlands (some 140,000 people) was wiped out during the Nazi occupation in the Second World War. Today, many Jews have returned to areas of Amsterdam. Anne Frank, the teenage Jewish girl who wrote a famous diary while hiding from the Nazis, lived in the city, and the house where she and her family lived in secret can be visited.

▲ *Dutch Hare Krishna followers being married in a Hare Krishna temple in neighbouring Belgium. Although the main religions are still Protestantism and Catholicism, many Dutch these days do not follow any religion at all.*

Festivals, sports and leisure

There are many festivals in the Netherlands, such as Queen's Day on 30 April. In Zeeland there are medieval Ringrijden festivals where people ride on horseback along a track and spear a small ring with a lance.

◀ *This is part of the traditional Ringrijden competitions in Middelburg Zeeland.*

National sports include speed skating and football. Dutch footballers play in teams all over the world. Ice-skating and cycling are also popular sports as well as windsurfing, swimming and sailing.

The computer has altered Dutch home life. Electronic games are very popular and people of all ages spend a lot of time on the Internet. Over 90 per cent of all homes have a computer.

▲ *The Lenten carnival at Maastricht takes place in the south of the Netherlands in the predominantly Christian provinces.*

IN THEIR OWN WORDS

'My name is Jantiena Dijkstra and I am a psychology student. I come from Oude-Bildtzijl in Friesland. Since the age of 6, I have played an old traditional Frisian ball game called Kaats. The game is played on a field by teams of three players, one server and two field-players. The ball is hit with the hand. But we wear gloves of course. Each time the ball is returned to a specific point, *kaatsen* are scored. That is how the game is won or lost. We have matches at the weekend in different villages. Most of the people in the area speak Frisian, which is considered to be the closest language to English.'

8

Changes at Work

Industrial production

Some of the traditional industries for which the Netherlands is famous, such as diamond cutting in Amsterdam and high-quality porcelain production at Delft, continue to thrive in the modern economy. An important industrial activity is the production of secondary products, in other words any product made out of an imported primary product. Primary products such as crude oil, iron and wheat for example are turned into secondary products such as petrol, steel and bread. Secondary products can be anything from computers to jet engines, from roasting and packing of Columbian coffee beans to making cosmetics from imported fish oils. This sector is now the second biggest income earner after gas and oil. There has been a shift into more automated industries, and into a large national and international service sector.

▲ *A porcelain and ceramics stall in the market at Delft. Antique Delft porcelain is highly priced in auctions throughout the world.*

One of the reasons for the Netherlands' economic success is the 'poldermodel' of industrial relations. This is a term describing the civilized way in which government, management and workforce sort out disputes and plan together for the future. Dutch companies such as Philips, Shell, Unilever, ING, ABN-Amro, Fokker, KLM, Elsevier and C&A are famous worldwide and provide ample proof of the success of Dutch business.

▶ *Unilever's new headquarters (the round tower) in Rotterdam. The Netherlands has a strong position in world trade.*

IN THEIR OWN WORDS

'My name is Con Bracke, I am 44 years old. I have worked at one of the Philips plants in Eindhoven for several years. I am a DVD software test engineer for their consumer electronic branch. As an employee of the company I have many benefits. I can use the plant's own sports centre and fitness club. We earn generally good salaries and have good job security … but for how long? These days Philips is moving a lot of production elsewhere in the world, where labour costs are cheaper. We have a famous local football team, PSV Eindhoven, who are sponsored by Philips and their stadium is called the 'Philips Stadium.'

Europoort

The importance of Rotterdam's Europoort cannot be overlooked. It has had a very significant effect on the economy of the Netherlands. This port facility of some 3,560 hectares, which was built between 1958 and 1978, is the largest in the world. There are five oil refineries in the Europoort alone. It is a highly efficient port, turning around the largest tonnage in the shortest time. It has attracted much business and industry to the Netherlands, such as shipping, trucking and transport.

◄ *A fuel barge travels through the Calland Channel in the Europoort industrial harbour complex, which is the largest in the world.*

Changes in the country

Farming practices are changing rapidly. The small, efficient family-owned farms have become highly automated. Wind power is being used widely. One wind turbine can produce a farm's entire energy requirements. Also, the computer has become an important tool for farmers, for managing, planning and selling their stock and products.

Since the 1990s the Dutch livestock industry has been hit by several outbreaks of animal diseases. There are concerns that intensive farming methods, in which animals are kept close together and raised as quickly as possible, have contributed to this problem. More farmers are trying to farm in ways that cause less damage to the environment and produce healthier livestock. But this tends to be a more expensive way of farming. The giant food businesses push down the price they pay for farm produce so far that many people feel it is impossible to sustain safe farming practices.

▼ *There is an increase in organic farming methods due to the number of animal diseases seen in recent years.*

Tourism

Tourism is important in the Netherlands. Amsterdam, with its tree-lined canals, beautiful old buildings, museums and exciting nightlife, brings in millions of tourists annually. But there are many other beautiful historic towns like Leiden, Delft, Utrecht, Enkhuizen, Harlem, Zierikzee, Urk, Groningen and Maastricht. Many come to visit the magnificent tulip gardens at the Keukenhof and the flower auctions at Aalsmeer. Some come to the famous cheese markets at Alkmaar, Gouda and Edam.

▼ *Men in colourful costume carry huge cheeses on wooden sleighs to be weighed in the Town Square at Edam and then sold. The famous cheeses sell throughout the world.*

◀ *A tour boat on the Oude Schans canal in Amsterdam's picturesque 'Venice of the North' central area. People from all over the world visit this exciting city.*

Farmers are looking to tourism for new ways of making their businesses profitable. They now run cycling holidays with home-stays at old Dutch farmhouses and converted windmills. They also run canal and river trips across rural Holland.

▶ *The number of agricultural workers from 1980 to 2000 halved due to big changes in farming practices.*

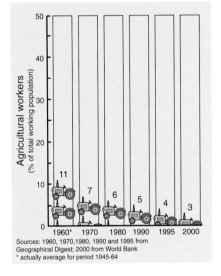

Sources: 1960, 1970,1980, 1990 and 1995 from
Geographical Digest; 2000 from World Bank
* actually average for period 1945-64

IN THEIR OWN WORDS

'I am Linda Pluimers and I'm 39. I work at one of the many bike hire shops in Amsterdam. I have worked here for three-and-a-half years now. It's great fun. I think that the centre of Amsterdam should be completely free of motor vehicles. Already much of it is. Bicycles are a way of life here – I don't know anyone who hasn't got one. Now all the tourists rent bicycles, because they have realized it is the best way to visit our city. I am single and Amsterdam is a great city for having fun. Maybe that is why we get so many tourists from all over the world.'

Changes to working life

Great changes are being made in the workplace. Since the 1990s, some industrial production has been moved to countries where workers' wages and raw materials are cheaper and taxes are lower. This is a change that has affected industries in many European countries. However, the Dutch economy has dealt with this change surprisingly well. The 'poldermodel' again succeeded and the workforce agreed to have their wages frozen. In fact the country has retained one of the lowest unemployment rates in the world. Very recently there has been a dramatic economic downturn. Time will tell if the 'poldermodel' will work this time.

▲ Clog making is a traditional industry, which is still thriving today because of the tourist trade.

IN THEIR OWN WORDS

'I'm Marisca Kensenhuis and I was born in Surinam. This used to be a Dutch colony in South America. I'm 32 years old and live in Amsterdam. I am a part-time stewardess for KLM so I visit the entire world. I also work in a café in old Amsterdam, mainly at the weekends. I love it there because of the great atmosphere, especially when the weather is good. Besides all this, I also do a full-time course studying communication management. I would like to be a copy-writer or journalist or work in Dutch television. That would probably mean moving to Hilversum, the town in Holland where all the television studios are located.'

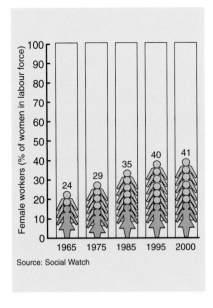

More people are now working as the government has reduced subsidies which previously allowed people to spend long years in further education, often changing courses and studying for as long as possible. From stable employment, where people worked in the same job for twenty years or more, they have now begun to move frequently between companies to get a better salary deal. Everyone is more mobile and much work is part-time. Many people feel this might undermine the traditional reliability of Dutch business.

Since 1970, more and more women have joined the workforce. However, 80 per cent of all key posts are still held by men, and women's wages are lower on average than their male colleagues. Many women in the Netherlands still opt for staying at home during the first few years of the children's upbringing, which affects their career opportunities in later life.

▲ *The number of women employed in the workplace has risen steadily since 1965.*

▼ *The number of women who work is increasing despite the fact that many men have higher paid jobs with more responsibility.*

New businesses

One positive outcome of the instability in the workplace is the opening of many new businesses. People who have worked for the same company for several years are often given large severance payments when they are made redundant and some choose to invest the money in new businesses. Opening a business has never been easy in the Netherlands. To start with, people have to have diplomas in accountancy, and then a diploma in the type of business they wish to conduct, for example, in hairdressing, or in food management for a snack bar. These rules ensure the customers receive a high standard of service. The tax authorities also have an easier time because even new entrepreneurs understand the principles of accounting.

The Netherlands has become a very computer-literate multi-lingual society. Both multi-lingualism and particularly computer technology have generated vast industries of their own: translation services, language schools and Internet-based companies.

▲ *These modern skyscrapers are part of the business heart of The Hague. Throughout history this country has been a worldwide trading power and is still a powerful trading nation today.*

IN THEIR OWN WORDS

'I am Yue Yan Wu and I am a Dutch national. I was born in China. I am a co-owner with my brother of a typical Dutch snackbar, or *frituur* as it is called down here in Limburg. My parents own a proper Chinese restaurant in Meersen. We are breaking with family tradition and cook Dutch snacks and of course French fries. We first emigrated to Europe when I was 12. That was to Italy. Then, when I was 17, our family moved to the Netherlands. So I speak Italian, Dutch, English, Putonghua Chinese and our own Wencheng dialect. As we are near the German border, I am also learning German.'

▲ *This Information Officer chooses images for a magazine. They will be scanned digitally and the layout of the magazine will be done entirely on the computer.*

European markets

The gap between European nations is closing fast, not only in practical terms such as laws and taxes, but also in the way they view each other. Most of the Dutch workforce is very highly skilled, confident in using information technology and able to speak other European languages. The Dutch are therefore more prepared than most to take advantage of new job opportunities across the expanding European Union. The introduction of the single European currency, the euro, has made it even easier for businesses to operate across Europe. The Dutch are perhaps the most pro-euro of all European nations.

▶ *GNP has risen dramaticaly since 1965. One reason for this is the money made from gas and oil supplies.*

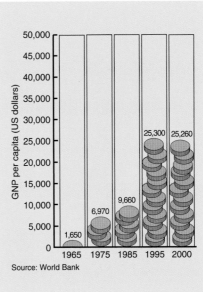

Source: World Bank

9

The Way Ahead

The Netherlands is a country that has fully embraced the European Union and its currency the euro, believing it to be essential for the future of an economically strong Europe. It is also in favour of closer co-operation between the countries of Europe. This closer union could finally bring the countries of Europe together in a new 'continent-country'. The hope is that this will ensure peace and stability for the future of the continent.

One consequence of the move towards closer European integration might be that the characteristics of individual countries become diluted. It is even possible that languages like Dutch will be replaced by a common language such as English for business purposes, with Dutch spoken only at home. On the whole, however, European union is seen as offering positive opportunities for Dutch people and the Dutch economy. The Netherlands and its Europoort will profit in terms of trade as other countries that are set to become part of the new Europe do not have the facilities of

▲ *Young people relax outside the famous Boymans-Van Beuningen Museum in central Rotterdam. Some of the greatest painters in the world are Dutch.*

◄ *The Dutch enjoy different styles of music from all over the world.*

IN THEIR OWN WORDS

'I'm Nathaly Archontaki. I'm 14 and I live in Maastricht with my mother. My grandparents live next door. My family is a living example of the European Union. My father is Greek, my grandfather is Spanish and my grandmother is Dutch. I speak four languages: English, Dutch, French and Spanish. I also speak the local Maastricht dialect. My hobby is flamenco dancing. I love it. Many Dutch people like it too. My grandfather emigrated from Andalusia in Spain to work in the coalmines here. Then they all closed, and after some other jobs, he and my grandmother opened a very successful tapas restaurant in the city. I want to become a European television presenter, broadcasting right across Europe from Dublin to Kiev.'

the Roterdam port. Already countries such as Poland, the Czech Republic, Slovakia and the Baltic States are already transporting their exports via the Netherlands. The future looks very bright indeed for this country. The Netherlands is at the heart of Europe with an eye on the wider world and it is a country that has changed in the past and is certainly ready to adapt to change in the future.

▼ *This is part of the 'Zeeland Delta Project'. In times of high tides and storms, the locks close, so that the sea is held back.*

Glossary

Apprenticeship The period of time a person spends learning a skill or trade in the workplace.

Automated industries Industries in which many or all of the processes are carried out by machines instead of people.

BSE Bovine Spongiform Encephalopathy – a disease affecting the brains of cattle, which can be transmitted to humans in infected meat.

Colony A country that is occupied and politically controlled by another country (countries).

Entrepreneurs Business people who are prepared to invest in new ideas in order to make profits.

Estuary The mouth of a river, where it flows into the sea.

European Economic Community An organization set up to promote trade links between some of the countries in Western Europe.

European Union A group of European countries that work together to achieve economic and social progress and strengthen Europe's role in the world.

Exports Goods that are sold abroad.

Genetically-engineered crops Crops that have had their basic genetic make-up changed in some way, for example, to make them more resistant to disease or produce a bigger crop.

Global warming The warming of the earth's atmosphere caused by the release of gases such as carbon dioxide.

GNP per capita GNP is gross national product, the total value of all the goods and services a country produces in a year, including investments in the country by other nations. 'Per capita' means 'per person', so GNP per capita is the total value of the goods produced, divided by the total population.

Immigrant A person who has come to live in a country from another country.

Imports Goods that are bought from other countries.

Life expectancy The average length of time that people can expect to live.

Mortgage Money that is borrowed from a bank in order to buy a house.

NATO North Atlantic Treaty Organization – an organization set up by the USA and Western European countries after the Second World War to defend the West against the military threat from the USSR.

Polder Land that was once under the sea but has been drained so that it can be farmed or built upon.

Porcelain A type of fine china.

Redundant Dismissed from work as no longer needed.

Service sector Businesses such as restaurants, banks and shops.

Severance payments Money that is paid to a worker as compensation for loss of employment.

Subsidies Money that is paid by the government to reduce the cost of, for example, producing goods.

Further Information

Books for younger readers

Vincent van Gogh:The Troubled Artist by Anna Claybourne (Raintree, 2004)

Festivals of the World: Netherlands by Joyce van Fenema (Times Editions Pte Ltd)

Cultures of the World: Netherlands by Roseline NgCheong-Lum (Times Editions Pte Ltd)

Van Gogh: Art and Emotion by David Spence (Ticktock Media, 1997)

Books for older readers

Here's Holland by Sheila Gazaleh-Weevers (Scriptum Publishers, 2001)

Anne Frank (People who made history) Edited by Jennifer Hansen (Greenhaven Press, 2003)

The Diary of Anne Frank edited by Christopher Martin (Longman Imprint Books, 2000)

Useful Addresses

Netherlands Board of Tourism and Conventions
PO Box 30783
London WC2B 6DH

Royal Netherlands Embassy
38 Hyde Park Gate
London SW7 5DP
Tel: 020 75903200
Fax: 020 72250947

Index

Page numbers in **bold** refer to photographs, maps or statistics panels.